CURIOUS CONUNDRUMS: 200+ ENGAGING RIDDLES FOR SMART KIDS

Fun, Puzzling Brain Teasers to Challenge Young Minds

2023
J S ALEXANDER

Contents

Superhero Riddles 2

Sports Riddles 5

Animal Riddles 8

Geography Riddles.. 11

Food Riddles 14

Music Riddles 17

Silly Rhyming Riddles 20

Gross Riddles 23

Movie Riddles 26

History Riddles 29

Maths Riddles 32

Magic Riddles 34

More Geography Riddles 37

Under the Sea Riddles 40

Toy-themed Riddles 43

School Riddles... 46

Super Short Animal Riddles 49

Famous Character Riddles 51

Dessert Riddles 54

Nature Riddles 57

Really Really Hard Riddles 60

Answers 63

Superhero Riddles

Riddle 1:

I have no superpowers, but I'm a hero still,

Gotham is where I live, fighting for justice.

You'll find me in a cave or mansion.

Who am I?

Riddle 2:

I'm a mutant with claws, known for my rage,

My healing factor keeps me on the stage.

I'm the best at what I do, without a doubt,

With my strength, I'm hard to take out.

Who am I?

Riddle 3:

I'm a man of iron, a genius in my own right,

With a suit of armour, I take to the sky.

Who am I?

Riddle 4:

Born on Krypton, I have powers grand,

With super strength and speed, I take a stand.

The symbol on my chest is a beacon of hope.

Who am I?

Riddle 5:

I'm a web-slinging hero, swinging through the air,

With great power and responsibility, I do care.

From New York City, I fight crime and save lives,

My spider-sense tingling, danger never thrives.

Who am I?

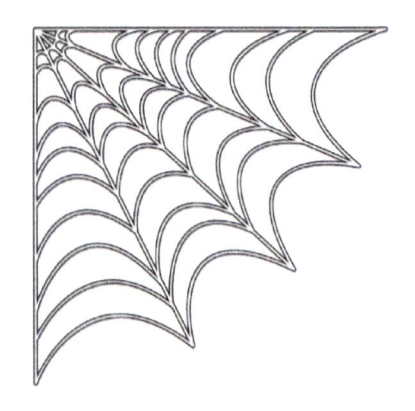

Riddle 6:

In tiara and bracelets, she takes a stand,

Justice she upholds with her mighty hand.

A warrior princess, fearless and bold,

Who am I?

Riddle 7:

I'm a green-skinned hero, with an emerald might,

Harnessing the power of a cosmic light.

With a ring on my finger, I shape constructs true,

As a member of the Corps, my willpower shines through.

Who am I?

Riddle 8:

I'm a mutant with telepathic might,

Reading minds, I see what's not in sight.

Leading the X-Men, I fight for mutant rights,

Using my powers to end humanity's fights.

Who am I?

Riddle 9:

I'm the god of thunder, mighty and bold,

Wielding Mjolnir, my trusty hammer.

From Asgard I hail, with lightning and storm,

Defending the realms, keeping evil at bay in any form.

Who am I?

Riddle 10:

I'm a stretchy superhero, with a heart so pure,

Bending and contorting, my powers endure.

Part of a fantastic team, fighting as one,

Invisible force fields and fire, together we're never outdone.

Who am I?

Sports Riddles

Riddle 1:

I'm a game played with a bat and a ball,

On a grassy field, we give it our all.

Hit it out of the park, or catch it in flight,

In this game, we play with all our might.

What am I?

Riddle 2:

I'm a sport played in water, you see,

With strokes and kicks, I set you free.

Dive in, make a splash, and swim so fast,

Competing in races, it's a watery blast.

What am I?

Riddle 3:

I'm a sport with a net and a shuttlecock,

Across the court, we hit and block.

Smash and serve, back and forth we play,

On the court, we strive to win the day.

What am I?

Riddle 4:

I'm a sport played on ice, cold and slick,

With skates on our feet, we glide and stick.

Slap shots and goals, we aim to score,

In this fast-paced game, we want more and more.

What am I?

Riddle 5:

I'm a sport played with a round ball,

Kicking and passing, we give it our all.

On a grassy field, we run and shoot,

In this game, teamwork is an absolute.

What am I?

Riddle 6:

I'm a sport played with a racket and a ball,

On a court, we rally and give our all.

Smash and volley, with backhand and forehand,

In this game, we strive to be grand.

What am I?

Riddle 7:

I'm a sport played with a disc in the air,

Throwing and catching, with skill and flair.

Frisbee golf or ultimate, we play with pride,

In the open field, we let it glide.

What am I?

Riddle 8:

I'm a sport played on a horse's back,

With gallops and jumps, we follow the track.

Dressage, jumping, or a polo match,

Equestrian skills we aim to catch.

What am I?

Riddle 9:

I'm a sport played with a small white ball,

On a green course, we swing and stroll.

Driving and putting, aiming for par,

In this game, we strive to be under par.

What am I?

Riddle 10:

I'm a sport played on a court with a hoop,

Dribbling and shooting, we jump and loop.

Slam dunks and three-pointers, with style we play,

In this game, we aim to win the day.

What am I?

Animal Riddles

Riddle 1:

I am big, strong, and love to roar,

With a golden mane, I'm known for sure.

In the grasslands, I proudly roam,

The king of beasts, I call it home.

What am I?

Riddle 2:

I'm a bird that can't fly high in the sky,

But I waddle and slide, oh my, oh my!

In the cold, icy lands, you'll find me there,

With a tuxedo-like coat, I'm beyond compare.

What am I?

Riddle 3:

I'm a creature with stripes, black and white,

In China, I'm a symbol, a delightful sight.

Bamboo is my favourite food, you see,

Climbing trees and munching happily.

What am I?

Riddle 4:

I'm a mammal with a long, sticky tongue,

Ants and termites, I slurp up as fun.

In the trees, I hang upside down,

With big eyes and a cute frown.

What am I?

Riddle 5:

I'm a colourful fish, so pretty and bright,

In coral reefs, I bring delight.

With vibrant scales and a swish of my tail,

In the ocean's depths, I gracefully sail.

What am I?

Riddle 6:

I'm a small creature with wings that flutter,

Pollinating flowers, a busy nectar-gatherer.

With bright colours, I am quite a sight,

Spreading beauty as I take flight.

What am I?

Riddle 7:

I'm a gentle giant of the sea,

Filtering water, gracefully I flee.

Warm-blooded and a massive size,

I feed on krill, a wonderful prize.

What am I?

Riddle 8:

I'm a creature that hops and carries a pouch,

With strong hind legs, I can surely vouch.

In Australia, you'll find me around,

Bounding and leaping, I never touch the ground.

What am I?

Riddle 9:

I'm a big animal with a trunk so long,

In the wild, with my herd, I belong.

Using my trunk, I can spray and drink,

Known for my memory, they often think.

What am I?

Riddle 10:

I'm a playful creature with a bushy tail,

Climbing trees, I never fail.

Collecting acorns and nuts so fine,

In the forest, I'm a friend of pine.

What am I?

Geography Riddles

Riddle 1:

I'm a famous tower, tall and grand,

In the heart of Paris, I proudly stand.

With iron lattice and a breathtaking view,

I'm a landmark loved by many, old and new.

What am I?

Riddle 2:

I'm a country known for kangaroos and koalas,

Vast deserts and the Great Barrier Reefs' wonders.

Down under is where I proudly reside,

With unique wildlife and beauty far and wide.

What am I?

Riddle 3:

I'm a river that stretches long and wide,

Through Egypt's desert, I gracefully glide.

Ancient civilizations thrived on my banks,

Leaving behind stories and remarkable ranks.

What am I?

Riddle 4:

I'm a mountain range, majestic and high,

With snowy peaks that touch the sky.

Stretching across several countries, you'll find,

Home to diverse wildlife and landscapes combined.

What am I?

Riddle 5:

I'm a city of dreams, where stars shine bright,

In California, I twinkle with delight.

Home to Hollywood and movie-making art,

Visitors flock to me, ready to play their part.

What am I?

Riddle 6:

I'm a continent rich in diversity,

With rainforests, deserts, and history.

From the Amazon to the Andes, you see,

Inca ruins and vibrant cultures are key.

What am I?

Riddle 7:

I'm a city of canals and gondolas,

Romantic vibes flowing through my plazas.

With stunning architecture and art galore,

In Italy, I enchant those who explore.

What am I?

Riddle 8:

I'm an island known for beaches and fun,

With luaus, volcanoes, and warm sun.

Surrounded by the Pacific's vast embrace,

A tropical paradise, a magical place.

What am I?

Riddle 9:

I'm a famous canyon, deep and wide,

Carved by a river with a relentless stride.

In Arizona, I am a natural wonder,

A sight that leaves visitors in awe and ponder.

What am I?

Riddle 10:

I'm a country of ancient history untold,

With pyramids, pharaohs, and treasures of gold.

Nile River's gift, where wonders endure,

A land that fascinates, mysterious and pure.

What am I?

Food Riddles

Riddle 1:

I'm a yellow fruit, sweet and bright,

Peel my skin to take a bite.

I'm packed with vitamins, juicy and fun,

A tropical treat enjoyed by everyone.

What am I?

Riddle 2:

I'm a vegetable that's long and green,

Crispy and crunchy, a healthy cuisine.

Add me to tzatziki or slice me up in a stew,

I add a refreshing flavour, it's true.

What am I?

Riddle 3:

I'm a dairy delight, cold and sweet,

Churned and frozen, a delightful treat.

With many flavours to choose and savour,

I'll cool you down in any flavour.

What am I?

Riddle 4:

I'm a popular sandwich spread,

Made from peanuts, smooth or chunky instead.

Spread me on bread, and you'll agree,

I'm a delicious snack for you and me.

What am I?

Riddle 5:

I'm a breakfast favourite, golden and round,

Served with syrup, a satisfying sound.

Fluffy and delicious, stacked up high,

A morning delight that makes you sigh.

What am I?

Riddle 6:

I'm a vegetable that's orange and sweet,

Rich in beta-carotene, a healthy treat.

Whether baked or mashed, in a pie or a fry,

I bring a vibrant colour to your plate, oh my!

What am I?

Riddle 7:

I'm a popular Italian dish, baked with care,

Layered with cheese, sauce, and flavours to share.

With toppings galore, from veggies to meat,

Every bite is a delight, so tasty and neat.

What am I?

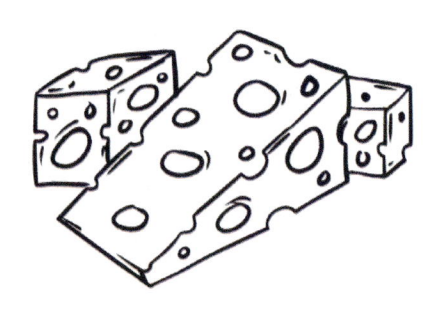

Riddle 8:

I'm a small and round fruit, red and juicy,

Perfect for snacking when you're feeling woozy.

Sometimes I'm sour, sometimes I'm sweet,

A burst of flavour with each little treat.

What am I?

Riddle 9:

I'm a classic beverage loved by all,

Bubbly and fizzy, I'll make you feel tall.

In flavours like cola or lemon-lime,

I'm a refreshing drink, oh so sublime.

What am I?

Riddle 10:

I'm a popular dessert, warm and gooey,

With a chocolatey centre, I'm truly chewy.

Served with ice cream, a delightful pair,

A dessert sensation beyond compare.

What am I?

Music Riddles

Riddle 1:

I'm a wooden instrument you can strum,

With strings that make beautiful music hum.

Pluck me gently or strum with all your might,

In melodies and chords, I take delight.

What am I?

Riddle 2:

I'm a metal instrument that you can blow,

With buttons and keys, my music will flow.

Hold me tight and press my keys with grace,

I'll serenade you with sounds all over the place.

What am I?

Riddle 3:

I'm a percussion instrument, fun and loud,

With a beat and rhythm, I make the crowd proud.

Hit me with sticks or use your hands to tap,

I'll add the groove to any musical map.

What am I?

Riddle 4:

I'm a small instrument, held close to your chin,

With bow in hand, the music will begin.

Strings I have, and notes I can play,

In an orchestra, I join the symphonic display.

What am I?

Riddle 5:

I'm a set of hollow tubes, of different size,

Strike me with mallets, a harmonious surprise.

Each tube produces a unique sound,

In an ensemble, I'm quite renowned.

What am I?

Riddle 6:

I'm a keyboard instrument, large and grand,

With black and white keys, an extensive span.

From classical to jazz, I can play it all,

Melodies and harmonies at your beck and call.

What am I?

Riddle 7:

I'm a brass instrument, shiny and long,

With a buzzing mouthpiece, I play my song.

Using valves or slides, I change my pitch,

In marching bands, I'm quite the hit.

What am I?

Riddle 8:

I'm a lively dance, a rhythmic affair,

With quick steps and spins, without a care.

In ballrooms or studios, I'll make you groove,

To the music's beat, you'll surely move.

What am I?

Riddle 9:

I'm a vocal style, a melodic expression,

With lyrics and harmonies, a musical confession.

Singing in groups or as a soloist,

With melody and emotion, I can't resist.

What am I?

Riddle 10:

I'm a musical notation, dots on a line,

Indicating pitch and rhythm, precise and fine.

Follow my markings, play the right notes,

In sheet music, I'm what the musician devotes.

What am I?

Silly Rhyming Riddles

Riddle 1:

I fly high up in the sky, with feathers that help me soar.

I hoot at night when others sleep, and hunt for mice galore.

What am I?

Riddle 2:

I'm a bright celestial body in the sky,

At night, I twinkle and catch your eye.

Far away, I'm a burning sphere,

A source of light, hope, and cheer.

What am I?

Riddle 3:

I'm yellow and bright, a radiant ball,

In the daytime sky, I stand tall.

I give warmth and light to all I see, the centre of our solar family.

What am I?

Riddle 4:

I'm a prickly plant, with spines all around,

Growing in deserts, where it rarely rains.

I store water within, in dry lands, where the heat is intense.

What am I?

Riddle 5:

I'm a box of wonders, locked up tight,

Full of jewels that sparkle and ignite.

In tales of pirates and adventures bold,

I'm the chest that holds treasures untold.

What am I?

Riddle 6:

I'm a vehicle with two wheels in line,

Pedal and steer, it's a fun design.

On streets and sidewalks, I ride along,

With handlebars and a bell, I'm never wrong.

What am I?

Riddle 7:

I'm a piece of clothing, cosy and warm,

Wrapped around your shoulders during a storm.

With buttons or zippers, I keep you snug,

In winter weather, I'm a comforting hug.

What am I?

Riddle 8:

I'm a container made of glass or plastic,

Filled with water, you take a sip fantastic.

In the fridge, I chill and wait,

Quenching your thirst, I'm simply great.

What am I?

Riddle 9:

I'm yellow and bright, a sunny fellow,

Peel my skin, I'm juicy and mellow.

In pies and smoothies, I taste so sweet,

A tropical fruit, a refreshing treat.

What am I?

Riddle 10:

I have hinges and a handle too,

I swing open wide for all to go through.

Knock on me when you want to explore,

I'm the entrance to what lies in store.

What am I?

Gross Riddles

Riddle 1:

I'm slimy and slippery, yet loved by many,

You'll find me in gardens, leaving trails aplenty.

Some people say I'm gross, but I'm not to blame,

I'm just a little creature, known by my slimy name.

What am I?

Riddle 2:

I'm sticky and stretchy, a bit of a mess,

When you squish me between your fingers, I impress.

I come in many colours, green, blue, and red,

Some might find me gross, but others use me for fun instead.

What am I?

Riddle 3:

I'm a tiny creature, crawling on the ground,

With many legs, people often find me quite profound.

I have a reputation for being creepy and gross,

But I help with recycling, so give me a little applause.

What am I?

Riddle 4:

I'm a food that's slimy, wiggly, and quite odd,

When you touch me, I might make you squirm and nod.

Some people think I'm yucky, but others find delight,

Especially as a dessert or snack, just right.

What am I?

Riddle 5:

I'm a smell that can make your nose scrunch,

Often associated with things that make you say "yuck!"

Though some might find me gross, there's a purpose I serve,

To warn you of danger and keep you on alert.

What am I?

Riddle 6:

I'm a bodily function that's often quite loud,

When it escapes, it can draw a crowd.

Some may think I'm embarrassing or gross,

But hey, everyone does it, even the most composed.

What am I?

Riddle 7:

I'm a substance that's gooey and sometimes green,

When you touch me, it's a sight to be seen.

I come from your nose, when you have a cold,

Some might find me gross, but I'm part of the body's mold.

What am I?

Riddle 8:

I'm a sound that can make you cringe and gag,

It comes from the throat, making everyone go "blah!"

Some may think I'm gross, but I have a purpose, you see,

To clear the airways and keep you breathing free.

What am I?

Riddle 9:

I'm a creature that's known for being quite vile,

With fangs and a hiss, I'll make you recoil.

Some may find me gross, but I play a role,

Keeping the rodent population under control.

What am I?

Riddle 10:

I'm a bodily waste that you can't ignore,

After digestion, I'm ready to explore.

Though I might seem gross, I'm a sign of health,

A natural process that occurs by itself.

What am I?

Movie Riddles

Riddle 1:

I'm a yellow creature, small and round,

With goggles and overalls, I can be found.

I speak in gibberish, but you understand,

In Despicable Me, I lend a helping hand.

Who am I?

Riddle 2:

I'm a toy, alive and full of wonder,

In a world of adventure, I never blunder.

With a cowboy hat and a faithful crew,

In Toy Story, I'll always be there for you.

Who am I?

Riddle 3:

I'm a princess with magical ice powers,

Creating a winter wonderland, hour by hour.

With a snowman friend, together we'll sing,

In a Disney movie that'll make your heart ring.

Who am I?

Riddle 4:

I'm a lion, the king of the pride,

In Africa's savannah, I'll always reside.

With my friends Timon and Pumba, we roam,

In a Disney classic, we find our home.

Who am I?

Riddle 5:

I'm a superhero with a red suit and mask,

Incredibly fast, my speed is hard to surpass.

Fighting crime with wit and humour in tow,

In a Marvel movie, I steal the show.

Who am I?

Riddle 6:

I'm a young wizard with a lightning scar,

Attending Hogwarts, where my journey starts.

With my friends Ron and Hermione, side by side,

In a magical world, our adventures collide.

Who am I?

Riddle 7:

I'm a little fish with big dreams to pursue,

In the vast ocean, I'll make my debut.

With a forgetful friend by my side,

In a Pixar film, I'll take you on a ride.

Who am I?

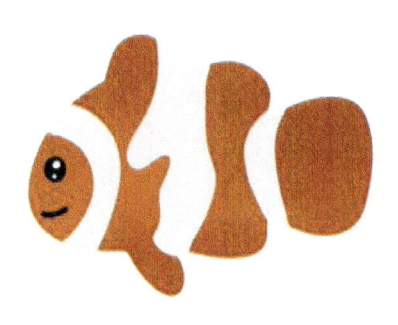

Riddle 8:

I'm a friendly alien with a glowing finger,

Lost on Earth, where wonders linger.

With a young boy, I'll form a bond,

In a Spielberg movie, our connection is beyond.

Who am I?

Riddle 9:

I'm a young girl with magical shoes,

Dancing my way through joyful hues.

In a musical movie, I'll tap and twirl,

Bringing enchantment to every boy and girl.

Who am I?

Riddle 10:

I'm a robot, a hero of futuristic might,

Saving the world, shining bright.

With my trusty friend, a cockroach small,

In an animated adventure, we stand tall.

Who am I?

History Riddles

Riddle 1:

I am a famous Greek warrior

who fought in the Trojan War.

My weakness was a vulnerable spot

on my heel. Who am I?

Riddle 2:

I am an ancient city in Italy

that was destroyed and preserved

by a volcanic eruption.

What city am I?

Riddle 3:

I am a legendary sword

associated with the story of King Arthur.

What is my name?

Riddle 4:

I'm an historical ship, on a fateful voyage,

Sailing across the ocean, seeking new age.

But destiny had a different plan,

As I struck an iceberg, a disaster began.

What am I?

Riddle 5:

I'm a famous inventor with a bright mind,

Electricity was something I defined.

With a kite and a key, a famous experiment,

My discoveries changed the world's sentiment.

Who am I?

Riddle 6:

I'm a legendary queen, wise and strong,

Ruling Egypt for decades long.

Known for my beauty and cunning ways,

A symbol of power that still displays.

Who am I?

Riddle 7:

I am an influential leader

who fought for India's independence

from British rule.

Who am I?

Riddle 8:

I am an historic event in the United States

that occurred on July 4, 1776,

declaring independence from Great Britain.

What is my name?

Riddle 9:

I'm an historical figure known for my dream,

A leader of peace, my words still gleam.

Fighting for equality and civil rights,

I inspired many with my powerful fights.

Who am I?

Riddle 10:

I'm an ancient civilization, steeped in myth,

Known for my pharaohs and hieroglyphs.

From the Nile River to majestic tombs and pyramids,

What am I?

Maths Riddles

Riddle 1:

I am an even number.

I am greater than 5 but less than 7.

What number am I?

Riddle 2:

I am a shape with three sides.

All my sides are equal in length.

What shape am I?

Riddle 3:

I am the number that comes after 9.

What number am I?

Riddle 4:

I am a number.

If you double me, I become 14.

What number am I?

Riddle 5:

I am a shape with no corners and no edges.

What shape am I?

Riddle 6:

I am a shape with four sides.

My opposite sides are equal in length,

and my opposite angles are equal.

What shape am I?

Riddle 7:

I am a number.

If you subtract 3 from me, the result is 9.

What number am I?

Riddle 8:

I am a shape with five sides.

What shape am I?

Riddle 9:

I am a number. Divide me by 2, the result is 4.

What number am I?

Riddle 10:

I am a number, so simple and small,

I stand alone, I'm the first of them all.

No other digit comes before me,

In counting, I'm as basic as can be.

What number am I?

Magic Riddles

Riddle 1:

I am a magical object,

used by wizards to cast spells.

With a flick and a swish,

I can make magic unfold.

Riddle 2:

I am a secret chamber hidden within a castle or a wizard's dwelling.

With ancient knowledge and treasures,

my mysteries are compelling.

What am I?

Riddle 3:

I am a legendary wizard,

known for my long white beard and wise counsel.

Many seek my guidance in times of need.

Who am I?

Riddle 4:

I am a powerful spell that can transport you in an instant.

From one place to another,

its magic is persistent.

What am I?

Riddle 5:

I am a magical plant known for healing,

with leaves that can cure wounds and pain.

Its properties are truly revealing.

What am I?

Riddle 6:

What am I?

I am a magical creature with wings,

granting wishes, small and mischievous.

Known for my magical stings,

What am I?

Riddle 7:

I am a mythical creature often associated with wizards.

I have the body of a horse

and the upper body of a human.

Riddle 8:

I am a school for young wizards,

where they learn and hone their magical skills.

Potions, Transfiguration, and classes to consider,

What is my name?

Riddle 9:

I am a dark and powerful wizard,

feared by many, a name starting with "V".

A name so sinister, many are too scared to say it out loud.

Who am I?

Riddle 10:

I am a legendary sword,

with magical properties, a wizard's reward.

Wielded only by the true, a name to be heard,

What is my name?

More Geography Riddles

Riddle 1:

A country with pride,

Eiffel Tower, croissants by its side.

The Louvre Museum, a treasure to see,

Which country in Europe could it be?

Riddle 2:

A land down under,

Kangaroos hopping, a natural wonder.

With koalas and Sydney Opera House grand,

What country's beauty is close at hand?

Riddle 3:

A diverse nation, North America's pride, a thrilling sensation.

Hollywood, Statue of Liberty standing tall,

And the Grand Canyon's awe-inspiring sprawl.

Which country am I?

Riddle 4:

Located in Africa's embrace,

With vast savannahs and ancient grace.

Home to the Great Pyramid, a marvel so grand,

In which African country do we stand?

Riddle 5:

Journey to a land in the east,

Samurais and sushi, a cultural feast.

Cherry blossoms blooming, a delightful hue,

Which Asian country is this clue leading to?

Riddle 6:

You'll find me in South America,

Home of the Amazon Rainforest,

Samba dance and Rio Carnival.

Which country am I?

Riddle 7:

A European state with castles, Oktoberfest,

a history so great.

The Berlin Wall's tale, a story untold,

Which country is this?

Riddle 8:

A Middle Eastern land,

Ancient ruins scattered across the sand.

Visit Petra and the Dead Sea,

Which country could this be?

Riddle 9:

I am located in Oceania's shores,

Islands aplenty, with cultural doors.

Maori heritage and landscapes so fine,

In which country do these wonders shine?

Riddle 10:

I sit at the top of North America,

Maple syrup, ice hockey and moose aplenty.

Niagara Falls, a majestic display,

Which country am I?

Under the Sea Riddles

Riddle 1:

I'm a tall plant with leaves so green,

swaying gently beneath the ocean scene.

What am I?

Riddle 2:

In the ocean blue, he's the hero of the sea,

With the power to communicate, who could it be?

He commands the creatures, big and small,

Protecting the oceans, answering the call.

Who is this superhero?

Riddle 3:

I'm not a fish, but I live in the sea.

With eight long arms, you can't catch me.

What am I?

Riddle 4:

I'm a graceful mammal, I love to swim.

With a blowhole on my back,

I make a splashy grin.

What am I?

Riddle 5:

I'm a slimy, squishy creature, without any bones.

In the sea, I slither and slide on my own.

What am I?

Riddle 6:

In the ocean's deep, where the waves gently sway,

There's a magical creature who loves to play.

With a fishy tail and long flowing hair,

She sings her songs with a voice so fair.

What am I?

Riddle 7:

I live in a pineapple under the sea,

With my best friend Patrick, oh so zany!

I work at the Krusty Krab, flipping patties with pride,

And my boss is a crab with a grumpy side.

Who am I?

Riddle 8:

In the ocean or on the sandy shore,

A reptile with a shell, steady and secure.

Slow and steady, it moves with grace,

Carrying its home from place to place.

What am I?

Riddle 9:

In icy waters, where it's cold and bleak,

A playful creature you may seek.

With a round body and flippers so strong,

On land and in water, it can belong.

Who am I?

Riddle 10:

I'm a special ship that dives beneath the sea,

Underneath the water, where fish are found.

I explore the ocean deep down.

What am I?

Toy-themed Riddles

Riddle 1:

I'm a cube and fun,

Twist and turn until I'm done.

Solve me by lining up my colours,

What toy could I possibly be?

Riddle 2:

Soft and sweet, a cuddly friend,

Given on special days with care to lend.

Comfort and warmth in every squeeze,

What toy brings joy and ease?

Riddle 3:

Roll and shake, numbers in view,

Guess the outcome, excitement grew.

A classic toy that brings delight,

What am I?

Riddle 4:

Bouncy and round, full of air,

Inflatable fun, beyond compare.

Jump and leap, have a ball,

What toy am I?

Riddle 5:

Wind me up, watch me go,

Moving toy, to and fro.

Characters and animals, a varied mix,

What toy is it? Take your picks!

Riddle 6:

Colourful pieces, a puzzling quest,

Arrange them right, put your skills to the test.

Create a picture, piece by piece,

What toy provides a brain-teasing feast?

Riddle 7:

Bricks and blocks, endless creations,

Building worlds, fulfilling aspirations.

Construct and imagine, with joy untold,

What toy lets your creativity unfold?

Riddle 8:

Remote in hand, ready for action,

Controlled movements, causing satisfaction.

Perform tricks, speed and spin,

What toy brings excitement within?

Riddle 9:

Throw, catch, and play,

Outdoor fun, a sunny day.

With friends, water splashing high,

What toy will make your spirits fly?

Riddle 10:

Float and glide, water's delight,

A toy that stays buoyant, oh so light.

Splish and splash, laughter's sound,

What toy adds wet adventure around?

School Riddles

Riddle 1:

I have pages and words,

but I'm not a book that you read.

You write on me with a pen or a pencil.

What am I?

Riddle 2:

I have a face but can't express emotions.

Students always watch me,

waiting for the bell to ring.

What am I?

Riddle 3:

I am a number that represents

how well you understand a subject.

The higher the number, the better your knowledge.

What am I?

Riddle 4:

I am a tool with a sharp point.

Teachers use me to write on the board.

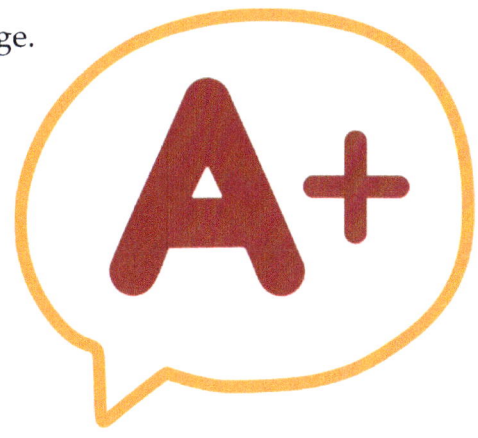

What am I?

Riddle 5:

I have four legs and a top,

but I'm not a table.

You sit on me and listen to the teacher.

What am I?

Riddle 6:

I am a room filled with books,

shelves, and knowledge.

Students come here to borrow and read.

What am I?

Riddle 7:

I am a group of students

who learn together.

We sit at desks and listen to the teacher.

What am I?

Riddle 8:

I am a colourful tool

that helps you draw straight lines and shapes.

Artists and mathematicians use me.

What am I?

Riddle 9:

I am a break between classes

when you can go outside, play, or have a snack.

What am I?

Riddle 10:

I am a small container

that holds pencils, pens, and other writing tools.

What am I?

Super Short Animal Riddles

Riddle 1:

What has a tail and fur but can't bark?

Riddle 2:

I am round and love the water.

What am I?

Riddle 3:

Swinging through trees, mischief in my eyes.

Bananas are my favourite snack.

What am I?

Riddle 4:

What has a trunk and big ears?

Riddle 5:

What has spots and roars?

Riddle 6:

What has a shell and crawls?

Riddle 7:

What has a beak and feathers?

Riddle 8:

What has a long neck and eats leaves?

Riddle 9:

I am black and white. I originate in Africa. What am I?

Riddle 10:

Four legs and a wagging tail, what am I?

Famous Character Riddles

Riddle 1:

I'm a princess with a magical touch,

Living in a castle, I love so much.

With a glass slipper and a fairy godmother's aid,

My story of love and kindness never fades.

Who am I?

Riddle 2:

I'm a lion with a mighty roar,

Ruling the Pride Lands, that's for sure.

I am brave and strong,

Hakuna Matata is my favourite song.

Who am I?

Riddle 3:

I'm a little mermaid, curious and bright,

Exploring the ocean depths day and night.

With a beautiful voice and fins so grand,

On land or sea, I'm ready to make a stand.

Who am I?

Riddle 4:

I'm a cowboy with a hat and boots,

Riding my horse, exploring routes.

In the Wild West, I'm the sheriff in town,

Keeping peace and justice all around.

Who am I?

Riddle 5:

I'm a fairy with wings so small,

Sprinkling pixie dust, I make dreams enthral.

In Neverland, adventures I bestow,

With Peter Pan, off to Neverland we go.

Who am I?

Riddle 6:

I'm a snow queen with powers so grand,

Creating ice castles with a wave of my hand.

In a kingdom of frost, I find my way,

Embracing love and thawing hearts every day.

Who am I?

Riddle 7:

I'm a toy spaceman, brave and true,

Fighting evil with my loyal crew.

In a world of imagination, we come alive,

With friendship and adventure, we strive.

Who am I?

Riddle 8:

I'm a young warrior, skilled with a bow,

In ancient Scotland, my tale will show.

With flowing red hair and a spirit wild,

I'll change my fate as a strong-willed child.

Who am I?

Riddle 9:

I'm a friendly monster with one big eye,

Studying at Monsters University, oh my!

Scaring kids is my mission and pride,

But deep down, kindness I can't hide.

Who am I?

Riddle 10:

I'm a genie in a magical lamp,

Granting wishes with a sparkle and a stamp.

With three wishes, you can ask for a delight,

But be careful what you wish for, day or night.

Who am I?

Dessert Riddles

Riddle 1:

I'm a tasty treat, soft and sweet,

Baked in the oven, a delightful feat.

With chocolate chips, I'm a favourite to eat.

What am I?

Riddle 2:

I'm a fluffy delight, a sugary cloud,

Whipped and frothy, I make you proud.

With flavours and toppings, a customizable dream,

In a bowl or a cone, I'm a creamy stream.

What am I?

Riddle 3:

I'm a dessert so grand, baked with care,

Layers of goodness, a delight to share.

For birthdays and celebrations, I take the stage,

With frosting and candles, I bring joy at any age.

What am I?

Riddle 4:

I'm a square delight, chewy and dense,

Made with oats and sugar, a perfect combination.

With chocolate chips, nuts, or dried fruit,

A snack or dessert, a tasty pursuit.

What am I?

Riddle 5:

I'm a round delight, a doughy creation,

With a hole in the middle, my perfect formation.

Glazed or sprinkled, I come in many flavours,

A breakfast treat that everyone savours.

What am I?

Riddle 6:

I'm a frozen delight, a chilly sensation,

Scooped in a cone, a perfect creation.

With flavours galore, from chocolate to mint,

On a hot summer's day, I'm a refreshing hint.

What am I?

Riddle 7:

I'm a small sweet treat, baked to perfection,

With frosting on top, a sugary connection.

I come in different flavours, vanilla or chocolate,

Sprinkles and decorations make me a delight.

What am I?

Riddle 8:

I'm a crunchy snack, a caramel creation,

Coated in buttery sweetness, a tempting sensation.

With a mix of popcorn and caramelized glaze,

A movie night treat that always amazes.

What am I?

Riddle 9:

I'm a frozen delight on a stick,

A colourful treat that does the trick.

When it's hot outside, I bring you cheer,

With fruity flavours that are oh-so-dear.

What am I?

Riddle 10:

I'm a creamy concoction, blended with care,

A frosty treat that's beyond compare.

Made with milk and ice cream, a delightful fusion,

Sipped through a straw, a sweet infusion.

What am I?

Nature Riddles

Riddle 1:

I'm tall and strong, reaching for the sky,

With leaves that rustle as the wind passes by.

In spring, I bloom with flowers so bright,

A symbol of nature's wondrous might.

What am I?

Riddle 2:

I'm a fluttering beauty with vibrant wings,

Visiting flowers for nectar it brings.

From flower to flower, I gracefully roam,

A symbol of nature's colours, I'm known.

What am I?

Riddle 3:

I'm a tiny home for buzzing friends,

Hanging high where nature blends.

Filled with honey, a golden treasure,

A symbol of teamwork and nature's measure.

What am I?

Riddle 4:

I'm a graceful creature with antlers on my head,

Roaming through forests, by nature led.

Majestic and regal, I stand tall,

A symbol of strength and nature's call.

What am I?

Riddle 5:

I'm a sparkling jewel on a clear night sky,

Shining and twinkling, way up high.

Constellations and galaxies, a cosmic display,

A symbol of wonder in nature's array.

What am I?

Riddle 6:

I'm a gentle droplet falling from the sky,

Bringing life to the land, as clouds pass by.

From rivers to oceans, I flow in a stream,

A symbol of purity, a nature's gleam.

What am I?

Riddle 7:

I'm a tiny creature that crawls on the ground,

With many legs, a curious mound.

In gardens and forests, I make my way,

A symbol of resilience, nature's display.

What am I?

Riddle 8:

I'm a natural wonder, so vast and wide,

With peaks and valleys, a breath-taking ride.

Home to diverse creatures, big and small,

A symbol of nature's grandeur for all.

What am I?

Riddle 9:

I'm a vibrant bloom, kissed by the sun,

With petals that open, a sight of fun.

In gardens and meadows, I bring delight,

A symbol of beauty, nature's colourful light.

What am I?

Riddle 10:

I'm a flowing body of water, serene and wide,

With fish and plants, a habitat's pride.

From lakes to oceans, I journey afar,

A symbol of life, nature's flowing memoir.

What am I?

Really Really Hard Riddles

Riddle 1:

I have a bright yellow face,

But I'm not the sun in space.

I tell the time with my hands,

Tick-tock, it never stands.

What am I?

Riddle 2:

The more you take,

the more you leave behind.

What am I?

Riddle 3:

I am full of holes,

Yet I can hold water.

What am I?

Riddle 4:

I'm round and bouncy, you see.

Kick me, throw me, catch me with glee.

But beware, I can have quite a blast!

Guess what I am, and the fun will last!

Riddle 5:

I am a colourful arc in the sky,

After rain, I'll catch your eye.

What am I that appears so high?

Riddle 6:

I am alive without breath,

And live below deck.

I am never thirsty, but always drinking.

What am I?

Riddle 7:

I am round like a circle,

With no end or beginning.

Spin me like cheese.

What am I?

Riddle 8:

I have a head and a tail,

But no body in between.

What am I?

Riddle 9:

I am tall when I'm young,

And short when I'm old.

I burn as bright as light.

What am I?

Riddle 10:

I can fly without wings,

Cry without eyes,

And see without a body.

I create dreams.

What am I?

Answers

Superhero Riddles

Riddle 1: Batman

Riddle 2: Wolverine

Riddle 3: Iron Man

Riddle 4: Superman

Riddle 5: Spider-Man

Riddle 6: Wonder Woman

Riddle 7: Green Lantern

Riddle 8: Professor X

Riddle 9: Thor

Riddle 10: Mr. Fantastic

Sports Riddles

Riddle 1: Baseball

Riddle 2: Swimming

Riddle 3: Badminton

Riddle 4: Ice hockey

Riddle 5: Soccer

Riddle 6: Tennis

Riddle 7: Frisbee

Riddle 8: Horseback riding

Riddle 9: Golf

Riddle 10: Basketball

Animals Riddles

Riddle 1: Lion

Riddle 2: Penguin

Riddle 3: Panda

Riddle 4: Sloth

Riddle 5: Tropical fish

Riddle 6: Butterfly

Riddle 7: Whale

Riddle 8: Kangaroo

Riddle 9: Elephant

Riddle 10: Squirrel

Geography Riddles

Riddle 1: Eiffel Tower

Riddle 2: Australia

Riddle 3: Nile River

Riddle 4: Himalayas

Riddle 5: Los Angeles

Riddle 6: South America

Riddle 7: Venice

Riddle 8: Hawaii

Riddle 9: Grand Canyon

Riddle 10: Egypt

Food Riddles

Riddle 1: Banana

Riddle 2: Cucumber

Riddle 3: Ice cream

Riddle 4: Peanut butter

Riddle 5: Pancake

Riddle 6: Carrot

Riddle 7: Pizza

Riddle 8: Strawberry

Riddle 9: Soda/Soft drink

Riddle 10: Lava cake

Music Riddles

Riddle 1: Guitar

Riddle 2: Flute

Riddle 3: Drum

Riddle 4: Violin

Riddle 5: Xylophone

Riddle 6: Piano

Riddle 7: Trumpet

Riddle 8: Dance

Riddle 9: Singing/Vocals

Riddle 10: Sheet music/Notes

Silly Rhyming Riddles

Riddle 1: An Owl

Riddle 2: A Star

Riddle 3: The Sun

Riddle 4: Bat

Riddle 5: Cactus

Riddle 6: Bicycle

Riddle 7: Coat

Riddle 8: Bottle

Riddle 9: Mango

Riddle 10: Door

Gross Riddles

Riddle 1: A slug

Riddle 2: Slime

Riddle 3: A worm

Riddle 4: Jelly or Jello

Riddle 5: A bad smell or stench

Riddle 6: Fart or passing gas

Riddle 7: Snot or boogers

Riddle 8: Cough

Riddle 9: A snake

Riddle 10: Poop

Movie Riddles

Riddle 1: Minion (from Despicable Me)

Riddle 2: Woody (from Toy Story)

Riddle 3: Elsa (from Frozen)

Riddle 4: Simba (from The Lion King)

Riddle 5: The Flash

Riddle 6: Harry Potter

Riddle 7: Nemo (from Finding Nemo)

Riddle 8: E.T. (from E.T. the Extra-Terrestrial)

Riddle 9: Dorothy (from The Wizard of Oz)

Riddle 10: WALL-E

History Riddles

Riddle 1: Achilles

Riddle 2: Pompeii

Riddle 3: Excalibur

Riddle 4: Titanic

Riddle 5: Benjamin Franklin

Riddle 6: Cleopatra

Riddle 7: Mahatma Gandhi

Riddle 8: Declaration of Independence

Riddle 9: Martin Luther King Jr

Riddle 10: Ancient Egyptians

Maths Riddles

Riddle 1: 6

Riddle 2: Triangle

Riddle 3: 10

Riddle 4: 7

Riddle 5: Circle

Riddle 6: Rectangle

Riddle 7: 12

Riddle 8: 8

Riddle 9: Pentagon

Riddle 10: 1

Magic Riddles

Riddle 1: Wand

Riddle 2: Chamber of Secrets

Riddle 3: Merlin or Dumbledore

Riddle 4: Apparition

Riddle 5: Mandrake

Riddle 6: Fairy

Riddle 7: Centaur

Riddle 8: Hogwarts

Riddle 9: Voldemort

Riddle 10: Excalibur

More Geography Riddles

Riddle 1: France

Riddle 2: Australia

Riddle 3: United States

Riddle 4: Egypt

Riddle 5: Japan

Riddle 6: Brazil

Riddle 7: Germany

Riddle 8: Jordan

Riddle 9: New Zealand

Riddle 10: Canada

Under the Sea Riddles

Riddle 1: Seaweed

Riddle 2: Aquaman

Riddle 3: Octopus

Riddle 4: Dolphin

Riddle 5: Eel

Riddle 6: Mermaid

Riddle 7: Spongebob Squarepants

Riddle 8: Turtle

Riddle 9: Seal

Riddle 10: Submarine

Toy themed Riddles

Riddle 1: Rubik's Cube

Riddle 2: Stuffed animal or Teddy bear

Riddle 3: Dice

Riddle 4: Bouncy ball

Riddle 5: Wind-up toy

Riddle 6: Jigsaw puzzle

Riddle 7: Lego

Riddle 8: Remote-controlled car

Riddle 9: Water balloon

Riddle 10: Pool float or Rubber duck

School Riddles

Riddle 1: Notebook (or Paper)

Riddle 2: Clock

Riddle 3: Grade

Riddle 4: Chalk/Whiteboard Marker

Riddle 5: Chair

Riddle 6: Library

Riddle 7: Classroom

Riddle 8: Ruler

Riddle 9: Recess

Riddle 10: Pencil Case

Super Short Animal Riddles

Riddle 1: Cat

Riddle 2: Bird

Riddle 3: Elephant

Riddle 4: Monkey

Riddle 5: Leopard

Riddle 6: Turtle

Riddle 7: Hippo

Riddle 8: Giraffe

Riddle 9: Zebra

Riddle 10: Dog

Famous Character Riddles

Riddle 1: Cinderella

Riddle 2: Simba, Lion King

Riddle 3: Ariel, Little Mermaid

Riddle 4: Woody, Toy Story

Riddle 5: Tinkerbell, Peter Pan

Riddle 6: Elsa, Frozen

Riddle 7: Buzz Lightyear, Toy Story

Riddle 8: Merida, Brave

Riddle 9: Mike Wazowski, Monsters Inc

Riddle 10: Genie, Aladdin

Dessert Riddles

Riddle 1: Cookie

Riddle 2: Whipped cream

Riddle 3: Cake

Riddle 4: Granola / Muesli Bar

Riddle 5: Donut

Riddle 6: Ice-cream

Riddle 7: Cupcake

Riddle 8: Caramel Popcorn

Riddle 9: Popsicle / Ice Lolly

Riddle 10: Milkshake

Nature Riddles

Riddle 1: Tree

Riddle 2: Butterfly

Riddle 3: Beehive

Riddle 4: Deer

Riddle 5: Star

Riddle 6: Rain

Riddle 7: Insect

Riddle 8: Mountain

Riddle 9: Flower

Riddle 10: River

Really Really Hard Riddles

Riddle 1: Clock

Riddle 2: Footsteps

Riddle 3: Sponge

Riddle 4: Ball

Riddle 5: Rainbow

Riddle 6: Fish

Riddle 7: Wheel

Riddle 8: Coin

Riddle 9: Candle

Riddle 10: Imagination

Printed in Great Britain
by Amazon

New York City Travel Guide 2025 by Carole J. Harvey is a complete resource for exploring the diverse offerings of NYC. This guide highlights the city's famous parks and outdoor spaces with detailed maps and images, making navigation easy. It showcases iconic landmarks, top restaurants, and cozy cafes for every taste.

Art lovers will find a curated list of museums and galleries, while those seeking culture can immerse themselves in Afro-Caribbean rhythms and the dynamic street art of Brooklyn. Designed for both first-time visitors and seasoned travelers, this book is your perfect companion for uncovering the essence of New York City.

ISBN 9798303323711